Fennec Foxes

by Jane P. Gardner

Consultant:
Blaire Van Valkenburgh
Professor
UCLA Department of Ecology and Evolutionary Biology

BEARPORT
PUBLISHING

New York, New York

Credits

Cover and Title Page, © Kim in cherl/Getty Images; 4–5, © Zhiltsov Alexandr/
Shutterstock; 6–7, © Juniors Bildarchiv GmbH/Alamy; 8–9, © Konrad Wothe/
imagebro/imagebroker.net/SuperStock; 10–11, © Paparico/Dreamstime.com; 12–13,
© Narit Jindajamorn/Shutterstock; 14–15, © Brett Bartek/Palm Beach Zoo; 16, ©
bikeriderlondon/Shutterstock; 16–17, © Claudia Harden/Palm Beach Zoo; 18–19,
© Ferderic B/Shutterstock; 20–21, © Hemera/Thinkstock; 22T, © Victoria Hillman/
Shutterstock; 22B, © Konrad Wothe/imagebro/imagebroker.net/SuperStock; 23T, © Brett
Bartek/Palm Beach Zoo; 23B, © bikeriderlondon/Shutterstock.

Publisher: Kenn Goin
Senior Editor: Joyce Tavolacci
Creative Director: Spencer Brinker
Design: Emily Love
Photo Researcher: Arnold Ringstad

Library of Congress Cataloging-in-Publication Data

Gardner, Jane P.
  Fennec foxes / by Jane P. Gardner.
      p. cm. — (Wild canine pups)
  Audience: 6–9.
  Includes bibliographical references and index.
  ISBN-13: 978-1-61772-925-6 (library binding) — ISBN-10: 1-61772-925-6 (library binding)
  1. Fennec—Infancy—Juvenile literature. 2. Foxes—Infancy—Juvenile literature. I. Title.
  QL737.C22G373 2014
  599.776—dc23
                                                    2013008957

For more information, write to Bearport Publishing Company, Inc., 45 West 21st Street,
Suite 3B, New York, New York 10010. Printed in the United States of America.

10 9 8 7 6 5 4 3 2 1

🐾 Contents 🐾

Meet a fennec fox kit 4

What is a fennec fox? 6

Where do fennec foxes live? 8

Finding food 10

A fox family 12

Newborns 14

Time to eat 16

Living in the desert 18

All grown up 20

Glossary 22

Index 24

Read more 24

Learn more online 24

About the author 24

Meet a fennec fox kit

It is a cold evening in a desert in Africa.

A fennec fox **kit** curls up on a patch of sand.

To keep warm, it wraps its bushy tail around its body.

The kit's father is out hunting for food.

Soon he will bring the baby something to eat.

fennec fox kit

What is a fennec fox?

Fennec foxes are the world's smallest foxes.

They are **canines**, along with wolves and dogs.

Even though they are tiny, the foxes have huge, pointy ears.

Adult fennec fox size

huge ears

Where do fennec foxes live?

Fennec foxes make their homes in the deserts of North Africa and Asia.

During the hot days, they stay cool in an underground **den**.

Atlantic Ocean

Europe

Asia

Africa

Indian Ocean

☐ Where fennec foxes live

N
W E
S

At night when it is cool, the foxes leave their den to hunt for food.

fennec fox leaving den

Finding food

Fennec foxes eat plants, and they also hunt.

They catch small animals, such as insects and lizards.

To find food, fennec foxes use their giant ears to hear animals in the sand.

Then they use their curved claws to dig up the **prey**.

fennec fox digging up prey

A fox family

Fennec foxes live in small groups called communities.

Each community has up to ten foxes.

community
resting near den

Sometimes two communities will live together in a large den.

Inside the den, the foxes are safe from enemies, such as owls and jackals.

Newborns

Each spring, a mother fox gives birth in the den.

She has one to five kits.

The kits are born with their eyes closed.

The newborns' eyes open after ten days.

fennec
fox kits

Time to eat

Kits drink their mother's milk for about three months.

After that time, they eat plants.

They also feed on small animals, such as grasshoppers, that their father brings them.

desert grasshopper

father giving food to kit

Living in the desert

At five weeks old, the kits explore the area outside their den.

Luckily, their bodies are built to handle the desert heat.

den

Fur on the kits' feet keeps them from getting burned by hot sand.

Their huge ears give off body heat to help keep them cool.

All grown up

The kits become adults when they are one year old.

Some of the foxes will stay with their parents' community.

Others will start a new community of big-eared fennec foxes!

Glossary

canines (KAY-nyenz)
members of the dog
family, which includes
pet dogs, wolves,
and fennec foxes

den (DEN)
a home where
animals can rest,
hide from enemies,
and have babies

kit (KIT)
a baby fox

prey (PRAY)
animals that are
hunted and eaten
by other animals

Index

Africa 4, 8

Asia 8

claws 10

communities 12–13, 20

dens 8–9, 13, 18

deserts 4, 8, 18–19

digging 10–11

ears 6, 10, 19

food 5, 10, 16

heat 8, 18–19

milk 16

mothers 14, 16

prey 10

size 6

Read more

Ganeri, Anita. *Fennec Fox (Day in the Life: Desert Animals)*. Chicago: Heinemann (2011).

Petrie, Kristin. *Fennec Foxes (Checkerboard Animal Library: Nocturnal Animals)*. Edina, MN: ABDO (2010).

Learn more online

To learn more about fennec foxes, visit
www.bearportpublishing.com/WildCaninePups

About the author

Jane P. Gardner is a freelance science writer with a master's degree in geology. She worked as a science teacher for several years before becoming a writer. She has written books about science, geography, history, and math.